FROM ASHES TO GLORY

FROM ASHES TO GLORY

How God Transformed Pain into a Revival of Faith, Unveiling My Purpose...

Genee C. Norbert

PCB

Published by Purple Chair Books and Educational Products, LLC

First Printing, 2025

Copyright © Genee Norbert, 2025

Norbert, Genee 1973-

From Ashes to Glory

ISBN: 978-1-953671-08-0

Christian Life/ Spiritual

Interior designed by Md Al Amin

Cover designed by Sadia A@Sadia_coverz

All rights reserved. No part of this publication may be reproduced, stored in a retrieval system, or transmitted in any form or by any means- electronic, photocopy, or recording- without the publisher's prior written permission. The only exception is brief quotations in printed reviews.

Dedication

To my son, **Blake Norbert**—this book is for you. For your children and your children's children. It is for all of the posterity that I leave behind.

From the moment I held you in my arms, I knew God had a divine purpose for your life. Every word in this book was written with that truth in mind—to pass on what I've learned, not just from Scripture, but from my experiences and suffering. From grace. From the depths of grief and the heights of God's redemption.

Throughout your life, I've tried to be an open book—to show you how to live, fall, and rise again, hurt and heal, surrender and trust. I want you to understand that discovering your *divine purpose* is the most critical pursuit you will ever undertake. Walking in that purpose will require trust, courage, and sometimes pain.

No matter what, son, please remember this: your pain will never be more significant than God's love for you. Ever! More importantly, if you hold on and cling to that truth— when the world feels heavy— you will make it through anything.

Your journey will be uniquely yours, designed by the God who knew you before I ever did. He gave you to me—and me to you—for a reason. Embrace that. Don't compare your life to anyone else's. Don't envy other roads. Accept your own, and walk it with faith, no matter how disconnected, non-linear, or complex it may seem.

God has a plan. Even when it doesn't make sense—even when it feels delayed or painful—**His plan** is always perfect.

Above all, trust **Him**. Trust Him with your whole heart. And don't let anyone make you feel like trusting God means you can't ask questions. It's okay to ask. It's OK to wrestle. That's how you grow. That's how you build a real relationship with Him.

If you veer off the path or find yourself hurting from your own decisions, don't run from God. Run to Him. Ask for forgiveness. Let Him show you who He created you to be because only God holds the blueprint for your life. And if you seek Him first, everything else will fall into place.

You don't have to chase approval. You don't have to chase success. Don't chase money—*chase God*. What He has planned for you is more significant than anything you could ever build.

Every challenge will carry a lesson. Every trial will have a gift. Every act of obedience will draw you closer to the man He created you to be. I pray that you live more than just a good life, but a God-led life filled with peace, purpose, and joy that doesn't depend on circumstances.

I pray that you grow to be a man who reflects God's love in words and actions. A man who walks in wisdom, courage, humility, and grace. A man whose life bears fruit for generations to come.

Blake, you are my greatest earthly blessing. My legacy begins with you. I am confident you will do amazing things.

With all my love— **Mom**

Table of Contents

Introduction 1

CHAPTER 1. Ashes and Awakening 3

CHAPTER 2. The Genesis of Revelation 7

CHAPTER 3. Seeking Answers in Life's Darkest Moments 13

CHAPTER 4. Why This Pain, God? 21

CHAPTER 5. Why Did They Leave So Soon? 29

CHAPTER 6. When Tragedy Strikes 37

CHAPTER 7. From Ashes to Purpose 44

Final Encouragement: Your Story Is Not Over! 54

🙏 Final Prayer 56

✝ A Final Blessing 58

Scripture Reference Guide 59

Additional Resources for the Journey 62

Introduction

"The Ashes That Awakened Me"

Seeking Answers in Life's Darkest Moments

As a pastor's child, I grew up in church and became familiar with many Bible stories. I identified as a Christian, but I realize now that I didn't honestly know God. I had not developed a personal relationship with Him that could sustain me through the profound losses I would eventually face. My faith was rooted in knowledge and tradition, but it lacked depth. When life unraveled—through unimaginable grief, heartbreak, and unanswered questions—I found myself searching for something more. I wasn't just seeking relief from pain; I was desperate for meaning, for truth, and for a hope that could anchor me through the storm. That search led me to open the Bible—not merely as a religious book, but as a lifeline. By reading Scripture and seeking God, I encountered Him in ways I had never experienced before. What I discovered changed everything.

What I have come to realize is that suffering, while deeply painful, is not without meaning. It can be where God reveals His most profound work in us. This book's heart explores how God brings purpose from pain and how the ruins of our lives—though marked by death, grief, and brokenness—can become the fertile ground where resurrection begins.

Throughout Scripture, *ashes* represent more than sorrow; they mark a threshold. Historically, people would sit in ashes to mourn or repent, acknowledging that something had come to an end. However, in the hands of a redemptive God, ashes signify the beginning of something new. They are not a sign of defeat but divine interruption, an invitation to transformation.

This book is my testimony from the ashes. Through the loss of loved ones, the grief that felt too heavy to bear, and the silent questions that haunted and rattled my faith, I have learned that God meets us in ruins. He does not waste our sorrow; He reshapes it into something sacred. Like Christ, who rose from death to life, we too are invited into a story of resurrection—again and again—as we walk with Him.

This is not a book of easy answers but one filled with honest questions, hard-won faith, and the hope that God is still writing a more remarkable story even when everything seems lost. In His hands, *ashes* are not the end; they are the sacred soil from which new life begins.

CHAPTER 1

Ashes and Awakening

Where Grief Begins, and Grace Finds Us

When you lose a loved one, whether suddenly or slowly—it feels as if the world keeps spinning while yours has come to a halt. The sounds around you continue, but inside, it's silent, a kind of silence known only to the grieving. I've dwelled in that silence more than once. This book was born in that silence.

I wrote these pages not as someone who has figured it all out but as someone who stands among the ashes—ashes of what I thought life would be, ashes of loss and heartache, ashes of unanswered prayers—and somehow discovers that even here, God is near, not just in the healing, not in the escape, but in the ashes themselves.

I've lost grandparents, parents, and even a sibling, all by the age of 37. Each loss imparted an unexpected lesson: suffering has significance. It's not a punishment; it's a pathway. And if you lean in—even when everything in you wants to run—you'll hear it too: I'm still here. I'm still working. This is not the end.

Pain shrinks and reduces us to our most authentic selves. It burns through pretense, exposes our limitations, and confronts us with questions we can no longer ignore. However, it also creates space—space for God to draw near, not always with explanations, but with His presence. Often, that's where new life begins.

This is not a book of simple answers. It is a collection of sacred struggles, Scripture held in weary hands, and prayers whispered through tears. Yet, it is also a book of rebirth—because on the other side of grief, if you dare walk through it with God, there is clarity, strength, and a deeper awareness of who you are... and even more, *why you are still here.*

If you're reading this, you've lost something or someone, even though your experience may not be identical. Perhaps you've lost your sense of direction or the life you envisioned. I want you to know this: you are not alone. The ashes you're standing in may be the sacred soil where your resurrection begins.

Let's begin

But before we move on, I want to linger a little longer on this image of *ashes*—because it has become more than a metaphor for me. Initially, ashes represented everything I had lost. They reminded me of what was no longer: the dreams, the people, the life I thought I would have. The ashes were a poignant reminder of devastation, mourning, and an undone life. However, with time—and only by God's grace—I began to see them in a different light. In the Bible, ashes are frequently associated with repentance and grief, yet they signify a turning point. They appear when something is over, true, but they also indicate the moment when God begins to act.

Ashes aren't merely what remains after a loss; they're what God uses to create something new. They are not debris to be discarded but a sacred invitation to transformation. Over time, I realized that God does not work around the ashes; He works through them.

He doesn't wait for the mess to be cleaned; He meets us in it. And when He does, He begins crafting something more beautiful than what was lost.

That's what I mean when I say resurrection begins in the ashes. The pain, confusion, and waiting—it's all part of the soil where God does His most mysterious and redemptive work. You are not behind or alone if you're standing in ashes right now. You are not forgotten. You are not disqualified. On the contrary, you are exactly where He's about to move.

Scripture for Reflection

Psalm 34:18 (NIV) — *"The Lord is close to the brokenhearted and saves those who are crushed in spirit."*

Romans 8:28 (ESV) — *"And we know that in all things God works for the good of those who love him, who have been called according to his purpose."*

Reflection Questions

1. What loss or moment in your life felt like it shattered everything you understood?
2. In what ways have you attempted to escape your pain rather than confronting it with God?
3. Can you recall a moment when you felt God's presence, even amid your suffering?
4. How might your pain be preparing you for something greater?

Journal Prompts

- Write a letter to God describing a moment when your life changed unexpectedly. Be honest about your feelings, what you lost, and what you still don't understand.
- Reflect on this: *"If the ashes I'm standing in are sacred soil, what new thing might God be preparing to grow?"*
- Meditate on Psalm 34:18. How does knowing God is close to the brokenhearted change how you see your grief?

Take your time. Be gentle with yourself. The healing process begins with honesty and is sustained by hope.

A Prayer to Begin

Heavenly Father,

As I open these pages and begin this journey, I carry with me all that I've lost, all that I don't understand, and all that still pains me. I may not have all the answers, but I know You are near to the brokenhearted. Lord, meet me in these ashes. Speak in silence, and show me that You are still working, even when I cannot perceive it. Please grant me the courage to be honest, the grace to rest, and the faith to believe that new life can emerge from this place.

May every word I read bring me closer to You. May each reflection help me uncover my purpose. May this be the start of something new, holy, and sacred.

In Jesus' name, Amen.

CHAPTER 2

The Genesis of Revelation

How the Cracks of Grief Opened the Door to God

If Chapter 1 was where the ashes settled, Chapter 2 is where I began to see what they were hiding: a holy invitation. The moment everything broke wasn't the end—it was the beginning. In the wake of unimaginable loss, I stood in the ruins of my faith, uncertain of who God was or whether I could trust Him at all. But what I've come to realize is that the breaking was sacred. It opened a path I hadn't seen before, not necessarily to answers, but a relationship.

Reflecting on my writings—particularly my childhood diary entries- I realize that I have always been deeply engaged in pursuing life's true meaning. Though well-intended, the Christian teachings of my youth did not fully capture the complexities of reality as I perceived them. The struggles, pain, and challenges I witnessed felt too intricate and complex for the seemingly simplistic explanations of faith. Disconnect left me frustrated, questioning how a sovereign God could allow suffering without providing necessary answers.

By the age of seventeen, I had lost my mother, who was an only child, along with her parents, the only grandparents I had ever known. One after another, they were gone, and it felt as if that side of my family had vanished overnight. With each loss, my questions intensified:

- Why was I enduring so much pain so early in life?
- How could a loving God allow this?
- What was my purpose on Earth?

I kept those questions to myself because I was told repeatedly, "Do not question God." But why? I pondered silently. Why was I not allowed to seek understanding if He governed my life? Was it sinful to ask?

The Struggle with Pain and Understanding

As I grew older, a deep sense of discontent settled within me. I continued to wrestle with the concept of suffering more than the actual events of loss. I couldn't reconcile how a sovereign, purposeful God would allow such suffering. I wanted more than clichés—I needed substantial understanding.

In 2006, my faith was shattered once again by my father's passing. A devoted pastor who had served for over 30 years, he was a pillar of wisdom, faith, and strength. Losing him felt unbearable. It was at that moment—the moment of my most tremendous grief—that I finally broke the rule. **I questioned God!**

In desperation, I cried out: "Why, God? Why so much pain? Why all this suffering?" Why did we have to endure another painful goodbye? Why were we forced to bury yet another parent while we were still young?

Watching my father and my mother deteriorate—watching them suffer—left me searching for answers in ways I had never done before.

The standard response many Christians give— "God knows best?" or the most repeated of them all, "He or she is in a better place"—felt hollow. I needed more than passive acceptance. I needed truth.

My search for understanding led me down an unexpected path. I realized my struggle wasn't just with suffering—it was with my lack of relationship with God. I grew up aware of God's existence and familiar with biblical stories and the lessons they taught. Yet, I lacked what was most essential—a personal relationship with Him. I knew about God, but I didn't honestly know Him. And without that relationship, my faith often wavered. With every loss, my heart hardened, and my inability to understand God had created a wall between us.

I realized that my lack of complete trust in God had quietly woven itself into every area of my life—my relationships, career choices, and countless other life decisions without seeking His guidance. I acted independently of Him because, deep down, I struggled to trust Him fully with my life.

Watching my parents suffer planted a seed of doubt that I found challenging to admit. I heard others testify about God's healing power and how He had restored them or their loved ones. But I didn't know Him in that way. He hadn't healed my loved ones on this side of heaven, no matter how much I prayed and begged, and in my spiritual immaturity, I couldn't recognize Him as this "healer" as others professed Him to be. He didn't care about my suffering or sadness. So, in pursuit of happiness, I mistakenly believed I had to create it, crafting my desired version of joy. You can only imagine the mess I made because of it. **But God!**

Reflecting on my past, I now recognize His grace and mercy

at work in every step. He tidied up every mess I created. In every pit I dug, He ensured I never toppled too deep. His patience and kindness were consistently present. Even when I strayed from His intended path for my life, He never abandoned me. Repeatedly, He has proven to be gracious and kind.

This book is my testimony of loss, grief, and transformation. It is a testament to how suffering and surrendering to God can lead to clarity, purpose, and renewal.

Whether enduring uncontrollable adverse life events or facing significant loss and hardship due to my own decisions, I understand that true faith, genuine joy, and profound understanding require more than passive belief. They necessitate actively pursuing personal knowledge of God's ways and developing a relationship with Him. Consequently, I began reading His Word independently. With each reading, every prayer, and intentional conversation with Him, it became increasingly clear that suffering is not without purpose. Through His word and time spent in His presence, the transformation began.

I didn't know it then, but those cries in the dark marked the beginning of a new kind of prayer. Not the polished ones I had been taught, but the desperate, broken ones that cause God to lean in close. I thought I was losing everything, but what I was genuinely losing was the illusion of control. I was being emptied, yes—but for a purpose. Because sometimes, before God rebuilds us, He allows everything not rooted in Him to fall away. That was the breaking point. And it was also where the real story began.

I now understand that pain can either defeat or develop us. While Satan may want to use it to harm us, God can use it as an instrument for refinement, fortification, and preparation for greater purposes. By sharing my experience, I aim to inspire others to seek a deeper connection with the Lord and discover meaning within their paths, regardless of their challenges.

Just as the ashes left after a burial became sacred, the remnants of my sorrow gained significance. The ground of grief was not barren—it served as soil for resurrection. As I began to seek Him, God started to plant purpose in what once felt lifeless and lost.

Scripture for Reflection:

- Jeremiah 29:13 (NIV) — *"You will seek me and find me when you seek me with all your heart."*
- Proverbs 3:5-6 (NIV) — *"Trust in the Lord with all your heart and lean not on your own understanding; in all your ways submit to Him, and He will make your paths straight."*
- Job 42:5 (ESV) — *"I had heard of you by the hearing of the ear, but now my eye sees you."*

? Reflection Questions:

1. How did your early religious experiences shape and influence your perception of God, particularly during pain?
2. What false beliefs or misconceptions did grief reveal in your life about God's nature or your worth?
3. Have you ever felt that you "knew about God" but didn't honestly know Him? What does a genuine relationship with Him look like to you now?
4. In what ways have you, knowingly or unknowingly, tried to take happiness into your own hands?
5. Can you identify a moment in your story when grace

intervened in your mistakes or misdirection, a "But God..." moment?

✎ Journal Prompts:

- Consider the walls that grief has built between you and God. Which bricks are made of questions, and which are made of silence??
- Write about a time when you questioned God—and instead of pushing you away, you found Him waiting.
- Reflect on Job 42:5. What has your suffering revealed to you about the true nature of God?

Closing Prayer: "The Genesis of Revelation"

Lord, Thank You for staying with me through the questions I was afraid to ask. Thank You for not turning away from my doubt but using it to draw me closer. In the places where I feel broken and confused, remind me that You are not afraid of my pain. Build something sacred in the cracks of my faith. Let my ashes become soil for something new. Teach me to trust You again—even when I don't understand. Amen.

CHAPTER 3

Seeking Answers in Life's Darkest Moments

When Questions Become the Beginning of Wisdom

When the foundation of my faith crumbled under the weight of grief, I found myself standing in silence, still calling out to God. Chapter by chapter, loss had been writing my story—but now, I was determined to reclaim the pen and begin asking the questions I had long been told not to ask.

This was no longer about mourning. It was about meaning. I had reached the point where easy answers and religious clichés were no longer sufficient. What I needed was something more profound and meaningful. I didn't just want to believe in God; I needed to know Him. To do that, I had to break a rule I had grown up clinging to and sheltering: *Don't question God!*

That realization didn't come in a single moment; it arrived in waves through countless tears and unanswered prayers. However, as I searched the Scriptures, I saw that I wasn't alone; the faithful have always questioned God. Job questioned His justice. David cried out in distress. Habakkuk demanded to know why God allowed evil to prevail. Even Jesus, in His final moments on the cross, asked:

"My God, My God, why have You forsaken Me?" (Matthew 27:46)

God did not condemn any of them. Instead, He revealed Himself to them more profoundly. Their questions became pathways to deeper faith. That truth shifted everything for me.

Breaking the Silence

In my exploration, I learned that sincere questioning does not offend God; it invites Him. He welcomes our doubts when paired with a heart that genuinely seeks Him (Jeremiah 29:13). When we wrestle instead of walking away; He meets us with wisdom. As I began cultivating a genuine relationship with Him—not merely one built on tradition or routine—I discovered that even His silence was intentional. Every decision He makes is rooted in divine wisdom and eternal purpose (Isaiah 55:8-9).

My Spiritual Journey

The church felt like a spiritual gas station for much of my life. I attended when I was running empty, hoping to gain enough fuel to get through the next leg of the journey. Although I often left feeling temporarily empowered, that fuel quickly ran dry once I returned to real life. Eventually, I realized I wasn't alone in this pattern. Many Christians seemed trapped in a cycle of survival but not thriving, enduring but not evolving. We clung to faith like a life raft—grateful it kept us afloat, yet never learning to swim. That realization led me to ask more profound questions:

- Are we growing in our understanding of God?
- Are we embracing the fullness of His Word?

- Have we reduced His teachings to a one-dimensional message of survival?

I recall attending a large church in Maryland where the message consistently emphasized the importance of enduring hardship. One Sunday, I asked a fellow congregant why suffering was the theme in nearly all the sermons. She replied, "Because there are many hurting people in the world." Her words lingered. They were true—but incomplete. Yes, suffering is real. But is the Christian life intended to be solely about enduring pain until Heaven? Is there something more for us, even now, amid it?

The Purpose of Suffering

As I delved into the Word, I began to perceive suffering in a different light. Pain is not merely an interruption of God's plan—it's often a crucial part. Scripture started to come alive in a fresh way:

- Job suffered not as a punishment but to prove his faith and God's sovereignty (Job 1:8–12; 42:10).
- Joseph endured betrayal and imprisonment, but it positioned him to save countless lives (Genesis 50:20).
- Paul faced affliction to remain humble and to rely solely on God's strength (2 Corinthians 12:7–9).
- Even Jesus, the sinless Son of God, suffered not for His own sake but to bring salvation to the world (Hebrews 2:10).

I realized suffering wasn't the end—it often marked the beginning. It was the point where transformation began.

When "Hold On" Isn't Enough

I used to find comfort in phrases like, "Your breakthrough is coming" or "Just hold on." However, those words eventually began to ring hollow and became empty, especially during the darkest moments of my journey. Even well-intentioned leaders can fall short when encouragement is limited to future promises of Heaven while failing to equip us for enduring today. Yes, we hold onto the hope of Revelation 21:4 that God will wipe away every tear one day. But if our only hope is the afterlife, how do we survive—and grow—in the meantime?

I now understand that Scripture is not merely about surviving life until we reach Heaven. It is about living victoriously on Earth, even while suffering. It serves as a guidebook for transformation rather than just consolation. God's Word teaches us not only to hold on but also to rise.

These messages of endurance, though well-meaning, mirrored the early stages of my spiritual journey—a cycle of spiritual survival. However, as my faith deepened, I recognized that God provides more than just comfort—He grants clarity, growth, and wisdom for the wilderness.

Understanding the Difference: Believer vs. Non-Believer

Pain is universal. Both believers and non-believers experience suffering. However, for the believer, suffering carries eternal significance. It refines, strengthens, and draws us into a deeper intimacy with God (Romans 5:3-5; 1 Peter 1:6-7). Pain, grief, and suffering in the believer's life have intentional consequences and purpose.

For those who lack faith, pain can feel random and cruel,

prompting them to seek temporary solace while ultimately leaving them feeling empty. However, for those who hope in God, suffering is never wasted. It becomes the tool God uses to mold us into His likeness and prepare us for the glory that lies ahead. Unlike those who reject and turn away from God, we have a guaranteed and eternal hope. Because of His love, He is faithful, even to those who are sometimes unfaithful!

Trusting God Even in Silence

We all seek answers. However, sometimes God doesn't respond how we hope or at the time we expect. Trusting Him in silence requires faith that transcends feelings. It involves believing He's still working, even when we can't see it. Often, it is in His silence that He accomplishes His most significant and profound work.

Pain as Preparation for Purpose

God knows what needs refining in us. He allows waiting, testing, and even breaking not to harm us but to prepare us.

- Moses spent forty (40) years in the wilderness before he was ready to lead (Exodus 3:1–12).
- David was anointed king but spent years running, hiding, and growing before he wore the crown (1 Samuel 16:12–13; 30:6).

If their prayers for quick relief had been answered, they would have missed the preparation for their call. We are the same. Waiting is not a waste of time. The wilderness is preparation, not punishment.

From Questioning to Calling

Ultimately, my questions didn't drive God away—they drew me closer. I realized that pain isn't a detour from purpose; it's often the path leading to it. God uses our darkest nights to prepare us for our brightest callings. This isn't just my story—it's a mirror for anyone who has ever asked why. My testimony is not one of perfection or unwavering strength but of divine persistence—of a God who met me in the ashes, handed me the truth in the silence, and taught me that even the most broken chapters could be rewritten for His glory.

Grief shattered me. Not only emotionally but also spiritually. It unveiled a faith that had been inherited yet remained unembodied. While the breaking was painful, it also created room for something I hadn't anticipated: a deeper connection with God. The questions that once made me feel disqualified transformed into the very language of my prayer life. The silence that once felt like absence started to feel like an invitation to listen differently, to lean in more profoundly, to cease demanding answers, and to begin desiring presence. I realized that the transformation didn't start when I figured everything out; it began when I stopped perceiving I needed to.

Perhaps you've also experienced this, standing in the dust of what you believed was unshakable, only to realize that what you're standing on isn't a grave... it's solid ground. Holy ground. The kind where God performs His most extraordinary rebuilding, not despite what you've lost, but through it and because of it.

Through divine revelation, I began to fear the questions no longer; I welcomed them. I knew that if I brought them to God, He wouldn't turn me away, which changed everything.

A Look Ahead

As I continued to seek God, the next chapter of my journey became profoundly personal. It was not merely about spiritual struggle or unanswered questions but about loss. Deep, life-altering, heart-wrenching loss. The kind that takes your breath away. The type that alters everything.

What follows are the stories of the people I loved and lost—and how God revealed His nearness, mercy, and purpose even in their absence. I invite you to walk with me into those sacred spaces where grief encountered grace and ashes began to whisper of resurrection.

📖 Scriptures for Reflection:

- Jeremiah 29:13 (NIV) – "You will seek me and find me when you seek me with all your heart."
- Romans 5:3-5 (NIV) – "We also glory in our sufferings, because we know that suffering produces perseverance; perseverance, character; and character, hope."
- Isaiah 55:8-9 (NIV) – "For my thoughts are not your thoughts, neither are your ways my ways,' declares the Lord."
- Job 42:5 (ESV) – "I had heard of you by the hearing of the ear, but now my eye sees you."

❓ Reflection Questions:

1. What questions have you been afraid to ask God—and why?
2. How has grief challenged or deepened your faith?
3. Can you recall a moment when God's silence taught you something more profound than words could ever convey?
4. In what ways have you spiritually survived but not grown or evolved in your walk with God?
5. Do you see any patterns in your pain that might be preparing you for something greater?

✏️ Journal Prompts:

- Write a letter to God with the questions you've been holding back.
- Reflect on a season of suffering in your life. What has changed in your understanding of God since then?
- Describe a wilderness season. What has been stripped away? What was planted in its place?
- How can you begin seeking relief from pain and purpose through it?

🙏 Closing Prayer: "When Questions Become the Beginning of Wisdom"

God, I've wrestled with silence and questioned Your presence, but You never let go. Thank You for being patient with my process. Show me how to seek You, not just in my triumphs but in my tears. Help me turn my questions into conversations with You. And when answers don't come quickly, let peace take their place. Amen.

CHAPTER 4

Why This Pain, God?

Wrestling with Divine Purpose Through a Loved One's Suffering

I believed losing my mother as a teenager was the hardest thing I would ever face. However, nothing could prepare me for witnessing my father's suffering and slow decline.

The dust of my grief had barely settled when I found myself standing among the ashes once more—this time witnessing the slow unraveling of the man who had held our family together: my father.

Throughout my life, my siblings and I have endured profound loss, witnessing loved ones suffer in their final days. These painful experiences made us question God's presence and purpose in our suffering. At just 15 years old, I confronted the devastating loss of my only living grandmother, who passed away from a stroke. A couple of years later, my mother, 46 years old, succumbed to breast cancer after a grueling battle that ended on Good Friday in 1991. Watching her slowly suffer and eventually pass away in our home was the most traumatic experience of my young life.

As I prepared to graduate from high school just weeks after her passing, I struggled to comprehend why God had allowed such suffering. However, I wasn't alone in my grief. The following year, my last living grandfather passed away, with many believing he could not bear the loss of his wife and only child—my mother. It felt as if my family was disappearing before my eyes.

At one funeral, I overheard a family friend say, "*Those poor children, their entire family is passing away.*" Those words haunted me for years. I often wondered if she realized how deeply her comment pierced my sorrow. The weight of grief and the reality of her words was nearly unbearable.

A Father's Strength and Faith

Amidst this devastation, my father—a pastor of two churches and the assistant principal of my high school—stepped into an unimaginable role. He became mother and father to my younger brother and me, the only remaining minors in our household. He bore the weight of providing for us emotionally, spiritually, and physically, never complaining. I still marvel at how quickly he developed such a potent and natural maternal instinct after my mother's passing. It felt as though God spoke through him, offering me the comfort and guidance I desperately needed.

Isaiah 66:13 (NIV) — "As a mother comforts her child, so will I comfort you; and you will be comforted..."

On numerous occasions, it felt as though God spoke through him, providing me with the comfort and guidance I desperately needed. His wisdom and steadfast faith sustained our family and the congregations he served. He often said, "*Girl, you better stop depending on me so much before God takes me.*" I laughed it off in response, never believing that God would do such a thing. How could He? He knew my father was my only remaining parent.

With my mother gone, my father would help plan my wedding someday. He would walk me down the aisle and perform the ceremony—a dual role only he could fill. He would continue to be my rock and support system, celebrating the good times and steadying me through the bad. Little did I know I was about to embark on a journey that would test my faith like never before.

📖 *1 Peter* 1:6–7 (NIV) — "You may have had to suffer grief… These have come so that the proven genuineness of your faith… may result in praise, glory, and honor…"

A Second Encounter with Cancer

In 2004, my father gathered our family to share devastating news: he had been diagnosed with multiple myeloma, a rare and aggressive cancer. The painful memories of my mother's battle with cancer resurfaced immediately.

There are no words to convey the emotions I felt at that moment. Still, I believed God to be too gracious and kind to allow my father's fate to mirror hers. Undeniably, He understood the emotional damage we had endured. My father was only 70 years old and, most importantly, a devoted servant and faithful minister. I thought God would heal him and use his testimony to glorify His name. But despite our prayers and faith, his condition continued to worsen. His doctors were baffled. Every treatment failed. His cancer never went into remission. Yet, my father's faith remained unwavering. I will never forget the day he collapsed in the pulpit while delivering a sermon. Even as his body failed, his spirit stayed and remained steadfast.

📖 *2 Corinthians* 4:16–17 (NIV) — "Though outwardly we are wasting away, yet inwardly we are being renewed day-by-day…"

The Pain of Watching a Loved One Suffer

In the spring of 2006, his body began to shut down. Blood clots, internal bleeding, and rising complications pushed him to the brink. I watched him deteriorate—physically, emotionally, spiritually. I held his hand while he slept, swallowing tears so he wouldn't see my pain. I whispered prayers I wasn't sure God was hearing. "Why?" I cried in silence. "Why would You let him suffer like this?" Watching my father—my hero, my teacher, my covering—fade away broke something in me. And on April 19, 2006—Easter Sunday—he passed away.

Wrestling with God in Grief

After his passing, I prayed for comfort, but the silence lingered. I couldn't understand why a man who devoted his life to God would be allowed to suffer so profoundly. I recalled the warning: "Don't question God." Yet, I had to!

Finding Purpose in Pain

When I asked the question, it became the answer. God began to show me that pain carries meaning. It's not cruel or punitive; it serves a purpose. That purpose may not always lead to healing on this side of heaven, but it always brings transformation.

📖 *Romans* 8:28 (NIV) — "And we know that in all things God works for the good of those who love Him..."

It is not cruel; it is not punishment. It is purpose. And that purpose may not always lead to healing on this side of heaven, but it is always about transformation. This truth became the foundation of my calling: to help others recognize God's presence during suffering and to help them understand that God is not absent when we are in pain. He is present. He is working.

Theology of Suffering

I have heard countless times that God uses pain to shape us. But in the rawness of grief, those words felt like salt in a wound. I didn't want theology; I wanted relief. I wanted answers. But what God gave me was *Himself*.

In the quiet aftermath of my father's passing, I began to realize that suffering isn't something we can escape on the path to spiritual maturity. On the contrary, it is the very soil in which maturity grows. Pain became the catalyst that drove me to Scripture, to prayer, and to ask more profound questions about who God is—not who I was taught He was, but who He has always been. Over time, I saw how Scripture is filled with individuals who asked "Why?"—Job, David, Jeremiah, and even Jesus. Their questions didn't diminish their faith but revealed a deeper meaning. Suffering did not drive them away from God but drew them closer.

📖 Psalm 34:18 (NIV) — "The Lord is close to the brokenhearted and saves those who are crushed in spirit."

Through these biblical stories, I realized that pain is not a sign of God's absence—it often serves as the most unmistakable evidence of His refining presence. He was not punishing me; He was preparing me.

A New Calling Emerges

As God began to heal my heart, I felt a shift—the sorrow I once perceived as a sign of abandonment transformed into an invitation.

I recognized that I was not alone in asking these questions. There were others—countless others—suffering in silence, feeling isolated in their pain and unsure how to reconcile a good God with a broken world. With this revelation, I understood that this was my call, not despite the pain but because of it. Through God's ordained process, I discovered I was meant to walk with others through their grief, to sit with them in the ashes and remind them they are not forgotten. As a result of what I have been allowed to experience, I developed an unwavering conviction and understanding to share with others that the same God who walked with me through the valley would also walk with them.

The Ashes Speak

Before I could fully embrace this truth, God gave me one more glimpse into His sovereignty—an unexpected moment that would transform my understanding of His perfect plan.

It was during the planning of my father's funeral that my siblings and I discovered something we had never known. When my father was young, his uncle compelled him to attend the Easter Sunday service. He wasn't obedient then, and the family worried he was heading down the wrong path. Yet, on that very day, at Mt. Calvary Baptist Church in New Iberia, Louisiana, my father dedicated his life to Christ. Years later, he returned to that same church, Mt. Calvary Baptist—not as a member, but as its pastor, serving faithfully for the next thirty years. In a demonstration of His sovereignty and perfect will, what some might call coincidence, I can only describe as divine orchestration. Not only did my father serve faithfully for thirty years in the church where he committed his life to Christ, but he also passed away on Easter Sunday—the same day he devoted himself entirely to the Lord's service.

God's plan for our lives is good. Whether He chooses to heal or not, or whether His answers come as we hoped or in unexpected ways, His plan remains perfect. I had to accept that my father's purpose had been fulfilled and that God, even in grief, was revealing His glory. Grief didn't destroy me. On the contrary, it dismantled what I thought I knew about God and rebuilt something more substantial: trust. Not in outcomes but in presence. Not in answers but in a meaningful and intimate relationship.

The question that once tormented me— "Why did my father have to suffer?"—has transformed into a different question: "How can this suffering be redeemed?" This shift has allowed me to find purpose not only in my father's suffering but also because of it. In honoring my father's memory, I've discovered that sometimes, the most potent ministry emerges not from our moments of triumph but from our deepest wounds. In that discovery lies a profound truth: when we offer our suffering to God, He can transform it into a blessing for others.

Through my tears, I discovered my calling. Through my questions, I developed a deeper faith. And through my father's suffering, I found a God who does not spare us from pain but walks with us through it, redeeming every tear for His glory and our ultimate good. His suffering as our *Christ* was not in vain—it was the very act that secured salvation for all humanity.

I used to think ashes signified the end. Now, I understand they can also represent a beginning—the sacred ground where beauty emerges, not because the pain is gone but because God is still present. Much like Jesus died so that we might have life, sometimes it takes losing those we love most to awaken the life we are meant to live.

📖 Scripture for Reflection:

- Romans 8:18 (NIV) — *"I consider that our present sufferings are not worth comparing with the glory that will be revealed in us."*
- Isaiah 45:3 (ESV) — *"I will give you the treasures of darkness and the hoards in secret places, that you may know that it is I, the Lord, the God of Israel, who call you by your name."*

Reflection Questions:

1. Have you ever questioned God during a painful experience? What did you learn through that questioning?
2. In what ways has suffering altered your perspective of God?
3. Can you identify a time when God used your pain to draw you closer to Him—or to help someone else?

Journal Prompt:

- Write a letter to God expressing the questions you've been afraid to ask. Don't filter it, be honest. Then listen. Reflect on any impressions, memories, or Scripture that come to mind.

Closing Prayer:

God, I don't always understand Your ways. I confess that my heart still aches, and my questions remain. But I want to trust You—not just with my joy, but with my sorrow. Use even this pain to shape me, to draw me near, and to remind me that I am never alone. Let the ashes I carry become something sacred in Your hands. Amen.

CHAPTER 5

Why Did They Leave So Soon?

Finding Peace in Untimely Goodbyes

From the Ashes of Unfinished Dreams

Losing my father taught me to trust in God's timing—even when I didn't understand it. However, the loss of my mother compelled me to confront a deeper ache: the pain of a life that felt unfulfilled. Her death wasn't just sorrow—it was silence. A vacancy. The ashes of what could have been. While my father's passing gave me perspective on a life fulfilled, my mother's death confronted me with the pain of purpose interrupted—or so it seemed at the time.

When Time Is Stolen

Loss is always challenging, but it feels like robbery or theft when it happens too soon. My mother's death at just 46 years old haunted me for years. She passed away on March 31, 1991—Good Friday. That irony has never escaped me. It was a day symbolic of death and divine suffering. For me, it became a personal crucifixion—the day the most essential relationship in my life was severed by cancer. She left behind unfulfilled dreams, unwritten books, a growing family, and a daughter who desperately needed her—who was merely a teenager at the time.

A unique grief arises when life ends before it seems complete. I didn't just mourn her absence; I mourned her presence in the moments she should have shared with me: weddings, babies, bad days, first jobs, and tough choices. I mourned the laughter we never got to share and the guidance I never received as I grew from a teenager to a young woman and then to a more mature woman. In those moments, I often cried out to God—not just in sorrow but also in confusion and anger, wondering: What was the purpose of giving her life if You were only going to take it away so soon? Why allow this woman to pour so much into others only to snatch her away before she could enjoy the fruits of her labor? I carried those questions into adulthood like invisible baggage, unpacking them repeatedly in the solitude of my pain.

Living Through the Absence

The pain of losing her didn't end with the funeral; in many ways, it only began there. I felt her absence most deeply during life's significant moments. One month after her death, when I graduated high school, she should have been in the crowd, smiling with pride. When I started college, I needed her voice to soothe my fears. When I became a mother, I longed for her wisdom, tenderness, and reassurance that I was doing things right.

I'll never forget my first Mother's Day as a mom. Everyone celebrated with brunches and cards, surrounded by generations of women. I smiled in public—but when I got home, I cried alone in my bathroom. I was mothering from memory, imagining advice and silent prayers, asking, "Mom, what would you do?" These wounds kept reopening. There was no closure—only adaptation. I didn't "get over it." I learned to live with the void and silent space.

The Fragility of Shallow Faith

At the time of her death, my faith was built on routine rather than on a real relationship. I knew about God, but I didn't honestly know Him. I believed He existed, yet I didn't think He was involved in my life. I recited prayers without expecting answers. I sang songs in church but failed to live out their proclaimed hope. When I cried in pain, I didn't know how to listen to His response. In the silence, I did not feel comforted; instead, I felt abandoned.

Like many Christians, I inherited religion but not *revelation*. I believed faith meant suppressing emotion; however, Scripture reveals something different. When Jesus wept at Lazarus's tomb (John 11:35), He knew He would raise him from the dead, but He still took a moment to grieve. Reflecting on that moment later taught me something profound about life: grief is not a sign of weak faith; it is a sign of deep love, and God honors both.

The Bitterness of What Could Have Been

There were days when anger accompanied my sadness. I didn't just mourn my mother; I envied those who still had theirs. I remember attending a friend's wedding. Her mother stood beside her, beaming as she adjusted her veil, prayed, and laughed through her tears. I excused myself and went into the restroom, weeping silently in a stall. That experience, moment, and memory of joy were taken from me.

📖 Joel 2:25 (NIV) — "I will repay you for the years the locusts have eaten..." My mother would never get to experience that with me—and I would never get to experience it with her.

While parenting, I have often stared at my son and thought, "*She would have adored you.*" When he was sick, I longed to call her for advice. When he was thriving, I wanted her to see what her daughter had become. I wanted her to know that I had made it—and that her love had been strong enough to carry me.

I would do the mental math each year: She would be 55 today... 60... 70. Every imagined birthday served as a reminder that she was frozen in time while the rest of us aged without her. Ecclesiastes 3:11 says, "*He has made everything beautiful in its time. He has also set eternity in the human heart.*" That verse made me realize something important. We mourn deeply because we instinctively know this isn't how it was meant to be. Eternity is woven into our souls. That's why early death feels so wrong—it disrupts what we believe should last forever.

Dreams, Confirmation, and Eternal Purpose

Years later, God granted me something I hadn't anticipated—a dream that transformed my entire perspective on my mother's death. In the dream, she sat with another woman, radiant and healthy. She looked peaceful. Happy. Whole. She turned to me and said: "*Do you ever feel like you have more to do in Heaven than you do on Earth?*" Those words, that line pierced me. It completely flipped and transformed my perspective. What if I had been viewing her death only through an earthly lens? What if, from Heaven's perspective, her assignment wasn't cut short—it was completed?

In that moment, I was reminded of Philippians 1:21— "*For to me, to live is Christ, and to die is gain.*" I began to think that perhaps death wasn't merely an ending; maybe it was a transition, a doorway into the next phase of purpose. My mother wasn't inactive. She wasn't gone. She had just been promoted. Perhaps she had work to attend to in the Master's presence that was more pressing than what remained on earth.

Divine Timing and a Different Measure

For a time, I measured life by the yardstick of years. But slowly, God began to show me that years aren't the only measure of fullness. Jesus died at 33, which is young by today's standards. But His assignment was completed, and in three years of ministry, He accomplished more than most people do in a lifetime.

We say someone died "too soon," but Scripture reminds us in Ecclesiastes 3:1: *"There is a time for everything and a season for every activity under the heavens."* God doesn't operate on human clocks. His timing is both mysterious and perfect. I didn't understand that when I was a girl. But over time, through study, prayer, and relentless grief, I began to trust it. I realized and understood that God's plans and ways are more profound, expansive, broader, and higher than we can fully comprehend. Romans 8:28 became an anchor: *"And we know that in all things God works for the good of those who love him, who have been called according to his purpose."*

From Goodbye to Purpose

Today, my mother's death no longer defines me; instead, it has refined me. I no longer bear the unbearable weight of questioning why it happened so soon. Instead, I am confident that God understood what I did not. Her purpose didn't die with her; it lives on in me, the love I pour into others, the strength I carry, and the testimony I now share with the world. Her absence fueled my quest, which led me to a deeper faith I never would have known otherwise.

I am confident that she is part of that "great cloud of witnesses" in Hebrews 12:1— "*Therefore, since such a great cloud of witnesses surrounds us... let us run with perseverance the race marked out for us.*" She is more than a memory; she is a motivator- a silent cheerleader from eternity, urging me forward as I carry the baton she passed on. Her story wasn't cut short; it was divinely timed. Now, it's my turn to live with the kind of purpose she died with.

📖 Scripture Reflections

1. John 11:35 – "*Jesus wept.*"

    - A powerful reminder that even Jesus paused to grieve. He weeps with us.

2. Ecclesiastes 3:1 & 3:11 – "*There is a time for everything... He has also set eternity in the human heart.*"

    - God's timing is not our own. We are wired for eternity, which is why loss feels so unnatural.

3. Philippians 1:21 – "*For to me, to live is Christ, and to die is gain.*"

    - What if death isn't an end but a promotion into purpose?

4. Romans 8:28 – "*And we know that in all things God works for the good of those who love him...*"

    - A foundational truth to cling to in seasons of unanswered grief.

5. Hebrews 12:1 – *"Since such a great cloud of witnesses surrounds us... let us run with perseverance..."*

    - Our loved ones continue to influence and cheer us on from eternity.

Reflection Questions

1. What unspoken grief have I been carrying that still affects my daily life?
2. In what ways have I measured life (mine or others') by years instead of impact?
3. How have I seen God bring purpose from someone's seemingly untimely death?
4. Have I ever envied others for something I lost? What would healing look like in that area?
5. What would change if I genuinely believed my loved one's purpose was fulfilled—even if it ended sooner than expected?

Journal Prompts

- Write a letter to the loved one you lost too soon. Share the moments you miss most and what you wish they knew.
- Reflect on a time when grief felt too much to bear. What helped you survive? Where was God in that memory?
- Finish this sentence: "If I believed God's timing was perfect, I would..."
- Consider someone else's loss—how might your healing story comfort them?

🙏 Closing Prayer: "Finding Peace in Untimely Goodbyes"

Jesus,

You wept at Lazarus's tomb, so I know You understand this kind of grief. Help me grieve without guilt and hope without fear. I miss the ones who left too soon, but I believe you're still writing something beautiful about my life. Heal the parts of me that feel lost with them. Let their legacy live through my love, faith, and purpose. Amen.

CHAPTER 6

When Tragedy Strikes

Searching for God's Purpose in Unexpected Goodbyes

From the Ashes of Sudden Loss

Chapter 5 reminded me how some goodbyes come too soon. But nothing could have prepared me for the one that lay ahead.

Losing my brother was not just another heartbreak—it was shattering. While the deaths of my parents brought me to my knees, this loss leveled me to the ground. There was no warning, no slow unraveling, only the aftershock of absence. Amid that grief, I faced a new kind of silence that screamed. We had endured so much together. He had helped keep my life—and my heart—whole after our parents passed. Just when I thought I had learned to live with loss, I found myself in the *ashes* again. However, this time, the ashes felt colder and more resounding. Even in that devastation, God was not absent; He was sowing something I couldn't yet see.

A Bond Deeper Than Blood

Some people say siblings grow apart over time, but for us, loss forged our bond, making us inseparable. After our parents passed, my brother and I clung to one another. Being only two years apart, our bond grew even more profound. He was my other half, safe space and laughter during the darkest seasons of my life. We did everything together: traveling, celebrating holidays, raising our boys. When people joked, "Girl, you'll never get married because you and your brother are always together." I'd laugh. But the truth was, that comment carried weight. We were always together. It was us against the world. He often told me, "We may not have our parents, but we have each other." And we lived by that.

We laughed more than we cried and healed each other quietly. He had his way, and I had mine. He assumed the role of father for my son after my dad passed, taking both our boys on bike rides and camping trips and teaching them how to pray and how to be young men of faith. Witnessing his parenting and how naturally he filled the father's role healed something in me that had broken after losing my parents. So, when I lost him—when he was taken suddenly—it didn't just feel cruel; it felt like a violation of everything God knew he was to me… and to them.

The Day the World Stopped

My brother had always been healthy, showing no signs of illness. However, he had been complaining of stomach discomfort for a few days- nothing alarming, just mild discomfort that he brushed off. One evening, after lying down to rest, he suddenly woke up choking. In a matter of moments, he was gone, having choked on vomit in his mouth- sudden, violent, unthinkable. We had just spoken and laughed, as always. He was planning to take our sons out the next day—another small, beautiful memory in a life filled with them. Then came the call. The police officer's voice was calm but strange: "Is your brother on any medication?" "Does he have a history of illness?" "No," I answered. "Why?" "Your brother collapsed. You need to meet him at the hospital."

The 45-minute drive felt like the longest of my life. I kept replaying our last conversation, trying to suppress the panic in my chest. When I arrived and saw him—covered in cooling sheets, his skin an unnatural shade- I knew something was (horribly) wrong. I could hardly stand. The doctor informed me that his heart had stopped, he had lost oxygen to his brain, and the outlook was grim. I couldn't breathe. I couldn't understand. This wasn't just my brother; he was my best friend, a father figure to my son, and my joy when everything else fell apart. Now, he was slipping away before my eyes. This could not be reality. This could not happen again!

The Cruelty of Repetition

This couldn't be happening. I had already buried our mother and watched cancer slowly take my father. Now, I felt as though I was reliving that pain all over again, but it felt even worse. This grief was no longer mine alone; it was also about our sons. I could see the anguish on their faces—a kind of loss we both knew too well. Two young boys were being robbed of the guidance and influence of a strong male role model. Their young hearts were becoming all too familiar with death far too early, and I was back in the valley. I thought I had survived. Devasted, I kept asking God: *Why him? Why now? Why would you take someone so good, so loving, so needed? Why take someone who has already survived so much? Why would You even think of taking the one person who helped us all survive losing everyone else?* He wasn't just a brother. He was the glue left holding us together.

A Holy Week Surrender

Surprisingly, I realized something: it was Holy Week again. The same sacred time when my mother had died, my father passed, and now —my brother? I couldn't make sense of the pain, but I prayed something bold: *"God if he must go, take him on Good Friday or Easter Sunday. It's the only way I'll survive this. It's the only way I'll believe there's purpose in this pain."* To this day, I cannot explain the peace that washed over me. Not comfort, exactly—but peace, as if God said, *"I hear you."* And I knew—I had to let him go.

I went to his bedside with no one else around. Through tears, I held his hand and whispered, "Larry, if you need to go, it's okay. We'll be alright. I'll take care of the boys. You don't have to fight anymore. I love you." On Good Friday, the day I had asked for, he went home to be with the Lord. So, here we have it: my mother and brother's passing, Good Friday, and my father on Easter Sunday.

When Faith Doesn't Feel Enough

Even in a time of prolonged peace, my world was shattered. On some days, I found it impossible to pray. During certain nights, I struggled to catch my breath. I witnessed too many people I cherished leaving this world too soon. I had seen too many young boys shed the same hot and stinging tears I shed at their age. *God, how do I trust you again? Father, how do I explain to my son, his son, when I can't comprehend or understand it myself?* Psalm 34:18 says, *"The Lord is close to the brokenhearted."* But at that time, He felt far away.

Despite everything, I continued to talk to Him—some days angry, some days silent, but always present. I remembered Jesus weeping at Lazarus's tomb, even though He knew the resurrection was coming. The reality of that scene reminded me that God doesn't dismiss grief; He joins us in it. Slowly, I stopped asking, "*Why did this happen?*" and started asking, "*What now, Lord?*"

Conclusion: The Threshold of Transformation

There are no words powerful enough to describe my love for my brother. He was more than family; he was a lifeline, a constant presence when everything seemed to fall apart. I loved him fiercely, and the depth of that love made the loss even more painful.

After his passing, messages flooded in from people I didn't know- friends, neighbors, and even strangers whose lives he had touched. I discovered things I had never known about him, such as how he stepped up in emergencies, gave without being asked, and forgave without being prompted. He never held a grudge; his heart was as vast as his smile, and his quiet strength supported more people than I ever realized.

My brother's death shattered something within me, yet it also ignited something new. The surrender I experienced at his bedside marked the beginning of a new chapter I hadn't previously realized existed. In his passing, a seed was planted. Not a replacement—but a calling. The God who allowed staggering grief so many times in my life was also the God who would use it. He transformed every loss into a new purpose and every question into deeper faith. Although I still grieve, I no longer grieve without hope. Romans 8:18 reminds us, "*Our present sufferings are not worth comparing with the glory that will be revealed in us.*" I believe that now, not just in theory, but in truth. If you've lost someone suddenly, please know that you are not alone. Your pain is real but not lasting. Your questions and frustrations are valid, but so is the peace that God offers—even in the unthinkable.

I carry my brother in everything. His voice still echoes in my laughter. His legacy lives on in both of our sons. His absence shaped my ministry, but his life shaped my heart. He was taken suddenly—but his impact is eternal. Despite the pain, I found my next breath in this holy mystery of grief, reconciliation, and grace, and eventually—my next step.

Scripture Study & Meditation

- Psalm 34:18 – *"The Lord is close to the brokenhearted and saves those who are crushed in spirit."*
- Romans 8:18 – *"I consider that our present sufferings are not worth comparing with the glory that will be revealed in us."*
- John 11:35 – *"Jesus wept."*
- Isaiah 61:3 – *"To bestow on them a crown of beauty instead of ashes… a garment of praise instead of a spirit of despair."*

Reflection Questions

1. Have you ever experienced the sudden loss of someone you loved deeply? How did it affect your faith?
2. What have you learned about God's presence in tragedy or silence?
3. How has loss shaped your understanding of love, purpose, or eternity?
4. What part of your heart still needs to hear, "It's okay to grieve—and you're not alone"?

✎ Journal Prompts

- Write a letter to someone you've lost suddenly. What would you want them to know?
- Describe a time when you sensed God's peace in a situation that made no sense.
- Journal a prayer asking God to reveal the purpose He may be shaping through your pain.

Spiritual Practice:

- Take a moment of silence this week to sit with God. No requests, no words, just stillness. Ask Him to meet you there and begin planting healing in the places that still ache.

Let this chapter remind you that tragedy doesn't have the final word. Transformation can begin even in the shadows—and grief can be the holy ground where God plants something new.

🛐 Closing Prayer: "Searching for God's Purpose in Unexpected Goodbyes"

God of Comfort,

I never expected to lose someone so dear so suddenly. This kind of pain feels unbearable. But still—I believe You are with me. Thank You for showing up even in shock, even in silence. Strengthen me to carry their memory well. Use this pain for Your glory. Turn my mourning into purpose. Please show me how to live with open hands, ready to receive healing. Amen.

CHAPTER 7
From Ashes to Purpose

*How God Redeemed My Pain
and Revealed My Purpose*

The Final Chapter: Rising from the Ashes

As I write this final chapter, I reflect on the journey that has brought me here. From the early loss of my mother to the slow and painful passing of my father and the sudden, devastating death of my brother—my life has been marked by deep grief and unexpected goodbyes. Chapter by chapter, I have walked through the ashes of each loss. However, this isn't a story about death; each chapter is a story of resilience and resurrection.

Chapter 6 reminded me that tragedy doesn't always permit us time to prepare. However, it also revealed that God doesn't abandon us amid the rubble. Instead, He meets us in the ashes—not only to comfort us but also to transform us. In this final chapter, I can genuinely say that the ashes of my sorrow have become the soil of my purpose.

What Grief Left Behind

After the funeral, what remains once the calls slow down and silence sets in? For me, it was a pile of unanswered questions, fractured faith, and the painful residue of three enormous losses: my mother, my father, and my brother. It felt as if everyone who loved me the most had left. I carried their memories and pain like invisible weights—trying to keep moving, trying to stay strong, yet feeling spiritually and emotionally depleted. In that space—broken, vulnerable, and grieving—I didn't turn toward God. Instead, I sought whatever might numb the ache of pain.

Grief doesn't just break your heart; it disorients your sense of self. I was no longer a daughter or a sister; I lost sight of who I was. As a result, I began seeking comfort in all the wrong places without even realizing it.

The Search for Comfort in All the Wrong Places

When sorrow became too heavy, I reached for what was easy, like many others. I sought what felt good—anything that numbed the pain, even if only temporarily. I entered relationships I had no business being in—rushed, codependent, and emotionally unhealthy. I wasn't seeking love; I was seeking relief. I wanted someone to hold me through the nights that grief had hollowed. I longed to feel chosen, safe, and worthy. However, sadness and brokenness attract brokenness, and I found more pain.

Each failed relationship eroded my confidence, self-worth, and trust. I internalized a false and misguided narrative that I was either too much or insufficient. I was no longer just grieving for my family—I was grieving for myself. The woman I once was felt lost amid the rubble. Somewhere in all of this, I began to lean on alcohol—not as a solution, but as an escape. A distraction. A way to silence the inner ache without having to confront it. But God... These are two of the most powerful words in my story. God never gave up on me, even when I was running, even when I was numbing, even when I was searching for healing in all the wrong places—He was still calling me back.

I will never forget. Sitting in church, completely exhausted and spiritually depleted, one day, I asked aloud, *"Okay, God... what do You want from me?"* His answer came clearly: "**Hospice**." I nearly laughed. Hospice? After everything I had witnessed—after all the loss I had endured? "Why would You ask me to return to that place of pain?" His reply pierced me: "Who else would I send? You've been there. You've walked through the valley. You understand."

Hospice: Where the Healing Began

Obedient yet uncertain, I enrolled in volunteer training for hospice care. As I stepped into those rooms—filled with grief, transition, and sacred silence- I began to understand why. My suffering hadn't been in vain; it had prepared me to comfort others in their deepest pain. I could sit beside grieving daughters and say, "I understand." I could hold a hand, offer a word, and pray over a soul in transition—not from a place of theory but from the furnace I had walked through. 2 Corinthians 1:3-4 says, *"God is our merciful Father and the source of all comfort. He comforts us in all our troubles so that we can comfort others. When they are troubled, we can give them the same comfort God has given us."* That Scripture became my purpose. The hospice work was quiet yet holy. I wasn't just helping people die; I was assisting families in navigating loss without losing hope. In the process, God was healing me.

When Healing Comes Through People

God didn't just send healing through ministry; He sent it through people—living, breathing vessels of His compassion and care. They were His answer when I didn't know how to pray, His comfort, draped in laughter and loyalty. Friends never judged me for the choices I made while grieving. They didn't provide simple answers or superficial solutions. They wept with me, sat silently beside me, and walked into my mess, not to fix it but to stay with me. That kind of love—the kind that doesn't flinch in the face of brokenness—is sacred.

My childhood best friend, Alicia, was one of those precious gifts. She never turned away, not even when I couldn't recognize myself. She stood by me through every high and low, spiritual spiral and emotional storm—and still does. Her love has been unwavering, and her presence reminds me that I was never alone.

Tonya embraced me with hugs that made me laugh, reminiscent of my brother's warmth. We shared a similar grief, both having lost our mothers at a young age and later enduring the heartbreak of losing our brothers. Instead of judging each other, we created a safe space for one another's pain and discovered ways to laugh through our tears. She embodies joy in human form, reminding me that sorrow and laughter can coexist and that even shared suffering can transform into sisterhood.

Over the years, God has used Alicia and Tonya to remind me of His mercy—His tenderness, closeness, and unfailing love. When I couldn't feel God, I could feel them. Through them, I came to believe He hadn't abandoned me again. He didn't stop there. He continued to send others—some right before my brother's passing and others in the years since—who became spiritual anchors in my life. They not only supported me; they surrounded me with prayer, words, and quiet faithfulness.

Atiya, whom I met shortly before my brother's death, became a constant source of strength. She comforted me through failed relationships, reminded me of my identity when I questioned it, and acknowledged the anointing within me when I forgot it was there. Her words often came like divine appointments—arriving at the perfect moment, I was ready to give up.

First Lady Tamara Scott—my spiritual sister and source of balance. She embodies the yin to my yang. Our stories hold remarkable similarities, and our shared love for Christ and our passion for health and wellness have united us in a divine and intentional sisterhood. Her loyalty comforts my spirit, and her gentleness is God's whisper in human form.

Pastor Dave Scott, whose shepherd's heart led me back to still waters, guided me to God and walked alongside me on my journey. He encouraged, challenged, and reminded me that my voice mattered, this story mattered, and this book needed to be written—for both me and those needing to see God in their ruins.

Alicia, Tonya, Atiya, First Lady Tamara, and Pastor Dave—I thank you from the bottom of my heart for being the hands and heart of God when I had forgotten how to reach for Him myself. Thank you for recognizing the woman inside me, even when I was buried beneath my grief and mistakes. Thank you for praying for me when I couldn't pray for myself. Thank you for standing in the gap and *(loving)* me back to life. You were the embodiment of God's mercy, wrapped in friendship. You reminded me that healing doesn't always happen in an instant—but it always arrives through love.

From Death to Life: A New Ministry Emerges

As I continued to serve in hospice, something new awakened within my spirit. I realized that many people were not only dying from disease but also from years of neglect. Their bodies had endured decades of unresolved pain, unhealthy patterns, and disconnection from purpose. God told me, "It's time to help the living." He began to reveal that wellness is a form of worship. Caring for our bodies is not an act of vanity; it's a responsibility and stewardship. Scriptures like 1 Corinthians 6:19-20 came alive: "*Your body is a temple... honor God with your body.*" Additionally, Romans 12:1 declares, "*Present your bodies as a living sacrifice...*" This revelation led to a second ministry focused on physical, emotional, and spiritual wholeness. My wellness journey became an extension of my faith journey. God was inviting me to teach people how to live—not just long lives but fulfilling ones. He guided me on how to steward my body in ways that honored Him and benefited others.

Trust Me: The Thread Through It All

Reflecting on the journals I kept throughout my adult life—through losses, heartbreaks, setbacks, and seasons of confusion—one phrase consistently appeared in God's responses to my cries: TRUST ME! It was written in all caps across the pages of my pain. In every entry soaked with sorrow, disappointment, and frustration, I heard Him whisper: Trust Me. Trust Me when it hurts. Trust Me when it doesn't make sense. Trust Me when they leave. Trust Me when your heart is broken. Trust Me when you don't know how to start over. Trust Me with your story.

Reflecting on this now, I understand it clearly. God wasn't just asking me to believe in Him—He was inviting me to trust Him with everything: the losses I never chose, the pain I caused myself, and the parts of my life I thought were beyond redemption. Now I realize He was always at work, always redeeming and loving me forward, even when I was unaware.

Friend, if you hear nothing else from my story, hear this: God can use it all—every bit of it, every heartbreak, every detour, every disappointment, even the self-inflicted wounds. None of it is wasted. Your pain is never in vain. Your story is not random. Your suffering is not meaningless. Your life is a masterpiece in the making—crafted by a Master who is all-loving, all-knowing, and endlessly patient. If you surrender it to Him, He will take the broken pieces and create something beautiful. He will reveal purpose where you once saw only pain. And one day, when your race is run, you will hear the words from Matthew 25:21: *"Well done, good and faithful servant... enter into the joy of your Lord."*

When Trust Is Put to the Test

Trusting God in quiet moments can be easy; trusting Him when everything is on the line is another. After years of being overlooked at work, passed over for promotions, and constantly trying to prove my worth—patterns I also recognized in my relationships—God spoke to me again. Feeling frustrated and exhausted during a work trip, He whispered clearly to my spirit: "This will be your last."

A couple of months later, after another deeply disappointing work experience, God spoke even more clearly. It was as close to audible as I had ever experienced: "It's time to go." I was taken aback—go where? Then, He provided specific and clear guidance that stopped me in my tracks: "Submit your resignation for November 30." What was God doing? I didn't have a job lined up, no steady income, and nothing awaiting me on the other side except obedience. Yet, the peace that accompanied that instruction surpassed all understanding. I knew it was *Him*.

In my humanity, I hesitated and delayed my resignation for a month due to fear. I felt it in my spirit; I had allowed fear to overshadow my faith. So, I returned to God, repented, and sought His forgiveness. In His mercy, He met me once again with love and grace. True to His character and nature, God truly showed up. Within months, I found a new church home and a supportive spiritual family. My pastor— Pastor Dave—believed in my story and encouraged me to finish this book. By divine design, he was a publisher who helped bring my vision to life. At the same time, I launched my own health and wellness business, coaching others in personal training and nutrition, and it is flourishing. It is thriving not because I did everything perfectly but because I finally trusted God enough to let go of what was breaking me and step into what He was building for me.

I testify that I have been abundantly rewarded for my struggles. The ashes of my pain have transformed into beauty and been repurposed for a positive impact and outcome. What once felt like the end has become a powerful beginning and a resurrection—a divine turnaround. What started with loss has turned into a legacy. The pain I experienced gave birth to purpose. That same God is ready to do the same in your life.

Conclusion: God's Resurrection Story

I once believed my story was defined by what I lost, but now I understand it has been shaped by what God has restored. I thought my grief disqualified me, and I believed my brokenness meant I would never be whole again. I feared that my poor choices would forever leave their mark on me. However, God—through His mercy,

His Spirit, His Word, and His people—rewrote my story. Now, everything I do, whether in hospice rooms, ministry, or health and wellness, comes from a place of profound restoration. I don't live as someone who has it all figured out but as someone who has been rescued, refined, and recommissioned.

If you are walking through pain or carrying shame from your response, please hear me: God is not finished with you. Your grief does not disqualify you, and your story is not over. There is healing, hope, purpose, and a future of grace waiting to be discovered. I have walked through the fire and found God there. I have fallen and realized that His mercy still lifted me. I have been lost and found myself again—not in the mirror, but in His presence. This is my testimony; this is His redemption story.

📖 Scripture Study & Meditation

- Isaiah 61:3 – "...to bestow on them a crown of beauty instead of ashes, the oil of joy instead of mourning, and a garment of praise instead of a spirit of despair."
- Romans 8:28 – "And we know that in all things God works for the good of those who love him, who have been called according to his purpose."
- 2 Corinthians 1:3-4 – "...the God of all comfort... comforts us in all our troubles, so that we can comfort those in any trouble with the comfort we receive from God."
- Proverbs 3:5-6 – "Trust in the Lord with all your heart and lean not on your own understanding..."
- Matthew 25:21 – "Well done, good and faithful servant... enter into the joy of your Lord."

🧠 Reflection Questions

1. Have you ever sought comfort in something (or someone) that ultimately left you feeling more broken? What did you learn from that season?
2. In what ways has God spoken to you during your pain—whether through people, Scripture, or divine nudges?
3. Who are the people God has sent to support and love you when you couldn't help or love yourself? Have you thanked them or reflected on their role in your healing?
4. Are there areas in your life where God asks you to trust Him more deeply?
5. What would it look like for you to fully surrender your story to God, believing He can use *everything*—even the messy parts—for His glory?

✎ Journal Prompts

- "Looking back, I now realize that God was with me when..."
- "The ashes in my life that God has begun to turn into beauty are..."
- "I'm learning to trust God more deeply with this area of my life: _____"
- "A moment where I knew God was using my pain for a purpose was when..."
- "I believe God is calling me to step into my purpose by..."

Final Encouragement: Your Story Is Not Over!

Beloved reader,

If you've reached this point, it signifies that you've achieved something sacred—you've walked through the ashes. You've permitted yourself to confront grief, the questions, the silence, and the pain. That requires courage. That requires faith. As you stand on the other side of these pages, I want you to hear this clearly: Your story is not over.

The ashes of your life are not the final chapter; they may very well be the beginning of a resurrection. If you've lost someone, wandered through the quiet ache of suffering, and ever felt as though your purpose was buried beneath the weight of sorrow, let me remind you of what I've learned through it all: God does not waste suffering!

I've buried my mother, watched my father fade, and grieved the sudden, unthinkable death of my brother. I've made mistakes while trying to survive my grief and rebuild my life. Yet, in every loss, every valley, and every heartbreak, I found a God who doesn't just comfort us in the ashes; He meets us there, gently lifting us into new life.

Jesus walked through death so that resurrection could be possible—not only for Him but also for Us. Because of Him, we don't just carry crosses; we also share the hope of the empty tomb. He takes what appears to be the end and reveals that it was never the end. What seems buried is often the start of something new.

You are not just surviving; you are being renewed. You are not beyond repair; you are being restored. You are not forgotten; you are being called. So, embrace every scar, every tear, every chapter of life that attempted to write you off—and offer it to the One who conquered the grave. Allow God to transform your mourning into a movement. Let Him utilize your pain as the foundation for your purpose.

This book may be finished, but your rise has just begun. Ask Him now: "*Lord, what do You want to bring forth from these ashes?*" And then—Listen. Trust. Follow.

Resurrection isn't merely an event; it's a promise. You are not beyond restoration. You are not beyond calling. You are God's masterpiece—in progress, certainly—but already beautiful, already beloved. Now go. Rise. Walk in your purpose. Live your redemption story, and assist another person in discovering that through Christ, even what appears lost can be restored to wholeness.

 Final Prayer

A Prayer for the Journey Ahead

Gracious and Sovereign God,

Thank you for accompanying me on every page of this story—the pain, loss, questions, silence, and the gradual revelation of your grace. Thank you for being present in the ashes, holding me when I couldn't keep myself, and staying by my side, even when I doubted you.

As this book concludes, I ask You to open a new chapter in my life and the life of the person reading. May this chapter not be defined by suffering but instead filled with purpose. You have shown me that pain is not meaningless, that tears are not in vain, and that when brokenness is placed in Your hands, it transforms into sacred ground.

I pray that peace fills every reader's soul, especially those experiencing grief and those struggling with guilt, trauma, or unasked questions. Let them feel Your presence and reassurance. Help them understand that they have not forgotten that healing is still possible and that it is never too late to discover their purpose.

Help them trust *you* again—not with perfect faith but with open hearts. Let them know they are not disqualified; *your* mercy can rewrite even the darkest chapters.

Transform every scar into a story. Convert every unanswered prayer into an invitation. Change every broken place into an altar where Your presence resides. Assure them that their lives are not random. They are not ruined. They are not over. You are still writing, and what You write is always redemptive.

Grant them the strength to move forward. Bless them with the courage to speak the truth. Bestow upon them peace that surpasses understanding. Most importantly, draw them closer to You—not through perfection but persistence.

May the seeds of faith sewn in these pages take root in every heart. May resurrection string from the ashes. May their lives become living testimonies—of healing, hope, and holy redemption because You are not done with them, me, or this story. In Jesus name, Amen.

A Final Blessing

I pray that you leave these pages feeling comforted and awakened. May every part of you that once felt shattered hold a glimmer of restoration. I pray that you learn to trust that what seemed meant to break you has only made you more beautiful in God's eyes. May you carry forward the truth that your story still matters, your voice still matters, and you still matter.

May the grief you've endured deepen your compassion. May the tears you've cried soften your heart toward others. May the faith you've discovered carry you through every unknown ahead. And above all, may you always remember—you are not forgotten. You are not forsaken. You are deeply, endlessly, and eternally loved.

Go now in peace, strength, and purpose. Your healing has begun. Your story continues. And God walks with you every step of the way.

Scripture Reference Guide

The scriptures presented in this book serve as anchors of hope, revelation, and transformation. You are encouraged to revisit them during your personal study, prayer time, and reflection as you seek God through suffering and healing.

Chapter 1 – The Breaking Point

- Romans 8:18 – Present sufferings vs. future glory
- Psalm 34:18 – The Lord is close to the brokenhearted

Chapter 2 – The Genesis of Revelation

- Isaiah 55:8–9 – God's ways are higher
- Jeremiah 29:13 – Seeking God with all your heart
- 1 Peter 1:6–7 – Faith refined through trials

Chapter 3 – Seeking Answers in Life's Darkest Moments

- Matthew 27:46 – Jesus' cry on the cross
- Job 1:8–12; 42:10 – Job's faith and restoration
- Genesis 50:20 – Joseph's purpose in suffering
- 2 Corinthians 12:7–9 – Paul's thorn and God's strength
- Romans 5:3–5 – Suffering produces hope
- 1 Peter 1:6–7 – Trials prove genuine faith

- Revelation 21:4 – God will wipe away every tear
- Exodus 3:1–12 – Moses' calling from the wilderness
- 1 Samuel 16:12–13; 30:6 – David's preparation for kingship

Chapter 4 – Why This Pain, God?

- Isaiah 66:13 – God comforts like a mother
- 1 Peter 1:6–7 – Faith refined through trials
- 2 Corinthians 4:16–17 – Inner renewal through suffering
- Romans 8:28 – All things work for good
- Psalm 34:18 – The Lord is close to the brokenhearted

Chapter 5 – Why Did They Leave So Soon?

- Ecclesiastes 3:11 – He made everything beautiful in its time
- Philippians 1:21 – To live is Christ, to die is gain
- Ecclesiastes 3:1 – A time for everything
- Romans 8:28 – All things work for good
- Hebrews 12:1 – Surrounded by a cloud of witnesses
- Joel 2:25 – God restores what was lost
- Romans 8:18 – Present suffering vs. future glory
- Isaiah 45:3 – Treasures of darkness

Chapter 6 – When Tragedy Strikes

- 2 Corinthians 1:3–4 – Comforting others through our comfort
- Job 1:21 – The Lord gave and has taken away
- Isaiah 61:1–3 – Beauty for ashes

- Genesis 50:20 – What the enemy meant for harm
- 1 Corinthians 6:19 – Your body is a temple
- Romans 12:1 – Offer your bodies as a living sacrifice
- 3 John 1:2 – Health and soul prosperity

Chapter 7 – From Ashes to Purpose

- Proverbs 3:5-6 – Trust in the Lord with all your heart
- Romans 8:28 – All things work for good
- 1 Peter 5:10 – After suffering, God will restore you
- Isaiah 61:3 – A garment of praise for the spirit of despair
- Matthew 25:23 – "Well done, good and faithful servant"

Use this guide to go deeper with God. Let His Word speak freshly into your pain, questions, and purpose.

Additional Resources for the Journey

In these pages, you have traversed profound depths. You have grieved, questioned, wept, and wrestled—and through it all, I pray you have sensed God's closeness in a way that has transformed you. Yet, the journey does not end here.

Below are additional resources to support, encourage, and accompany you beyond the final chapter. Whether you are navigating new grief, rebuilding your faith, or stepping into your purpose, this page is here to assist you.

Grief & Emotional Healing

Grief Share – www.griefshare.org
Faith-based support groups for those mourning the death of a loved one.

The Compassionate Friends – www.compassionatefriends.org
Support for families grieving the death of a child or sibling.

Faithful Counseling – www.faithfulcounseling.com
Professional online counseling from a biblical worldview.

Spiritual Growth & Discipleship

YouVersion Bible App – Bible reading plans, devotionals, and tools for deeper study.

Daily Grace Co. – www.thedailygraceco.com

Beautiful resources to grow in Scripture and prayer.

Recommended Reading:

- A *Grace Disguised* by Jerry Sittser
- *It's Not Supposed to Be This Way* by Lysa TerKeurst
- *The Purpose Driven Life* by Rick Warren
- *Walking with God Through Pain and Suffering* by Timothy Keller

Community & Support

Find a Local Church or Small Group
Healing occurs within a community. Find a faith community that embodies love and teaches truth.

Start a Journal or Healing Circle
Use the prompts in this book to start a small group or begin a journaling journey with a trusted friend.

Stay Connected

If this book resonated with you, if you need prayer, or wish to share how God is moving in your life, I would love to hear from you.

Connect with Me:
Instagram: @snatchedandfit
Facebook: Snatched Fitness Center
Speaking Requests, Workshops, or Retreats:
thesnatchedandfitcenter@gmail.com

www.ingramcontent.com/pod-product-compliance
Lightning Source LLC
LaVergne TN
LVHW041236080426
835508LV00011B/1234